Africa WiLD!

GROOVY TUBE BOOK™

written by **SUSAN RING**

illustrated by **BERNARD ADNET**

Line art by Rosanne Kakos-Main
Game by Susan Ring
Copyright © 2000 by innovativeKids®
All rights reserved
Published by innovativeKids®,
a division of innovative USA®, Inc.
18 Ann Street, Norwalk, CT 06854
Printed in China
20 19 18 17 16 15 14 13

PHOTO CREDITS

Cover, pp. 4 top, 4 bottom, 8 left, 15, 18 left: © Gerard Lacz/Peter Arnold, Inc.; pp. 5, 14 right, 20–21: © S. J. Kraseman/Peter Arnold, Inc.; p. 6 top: © Doug Cheeseman/Peter Arnold, Inc.; pp. 6 right, 16, 17 top right, 18–19, 19: © Gunter Ziesler/Peter Arnold, Inc.; p. 7: © Manfred Danneger/Peter Arnold, Inc.; pp. 8–9: © Luiz Marigo/Peter Arnold, Inc.; pp. 9, 17 top left, 20: © Fritz Pölking/Peter Arnold, Inc.; p. 10 top: © Tompix/Peter Arnold, Inc.; p. 10 bottom: © N. J. Dennis/BIOS/Peter Arnold, Inc.; p. 11: © Roland Seitre/Peter Arnold, Inc.; pp. 12 left, 13, 14 left: © M & C Denis-Huot/BIOS/Peter Arnold, Inc.; p. 12 right: © Kevin Schafer/Peter Arnold, Inc.; p. 17 top middle: © C. Alan Morgan/Peter Arnold, Inc.; p. 17 bottom: John Warden, West Stock; p. 21: © Steve Kaufman/Peter Arnold, Inc.

Amazing African Animals

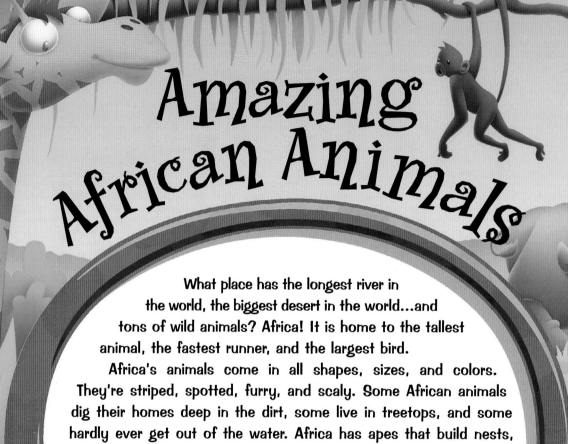

What place has the longest river in the world, the biggest desert in the world...and tons of wild animals? Africa! It is home to the tallest animal, the fastest runner, and the largest bird.

Africa's animals come in all shapes, sizes, and colors. They're striped, spotted, furry, and scaly. Some African animals dig their homes deep in the dirt, some live in treetops, and some hardly ever get out of the water. Africa has apes that build nests, leopards that swim, and birds that eat upside down. It has animals that graze all day and others that might eat only once a year. Some will even walk hundreds of miles for food and water.

Who is who, and which does what? Get ready to find the answers to these questions and meet some wild and most amazing African animals!

3

Home, Home on the Plain

The wide-open, grassy plains of Africa are known as the *savannah*. Many different types of animals make the savannah their home, and the lion is one of them. Lions deserve their title of king. They may fight with hyenas over food, but they really have no enemies.

Lions can bite through a large bone in one chomp. Most other animals leave lions alone. That is why lions can spend up to 20 hours a day stretching and snoozing under the hot sun or a shady tree.

Lion families stay together in a group, called a *pride*. The female lion, the lioness, joins other females in the pride to hunt. Male lions stay home to protect their territory and their cubs from other lions.

Above: A lion shows its strong teeth.
Left: This lioness is ready to pounce.

Besides those mighty hunters, giraffes, gazelles, and warthogs live on the savannah, too. Giraffes nibble leaves in the tree-tops, gazelles graze in the grass, and warthogs bend their front knees so they can kneel down to sniff out grubs and goodies in the dirt.

Left: A warthog kneels to find some food.

Isn't It Wild?

Warthogs are hunted by lions, cheetahs, and hyenas. But they have a very clever way of protecting themselves. When a warthog gets to its burrow, it does an "about-face" and goes in backward! The warthog's mighty tusks are facing outward—and those tusks are powerful weapons. So a warthog's enemies better think twice before following it into its home!

Deep in the Forest

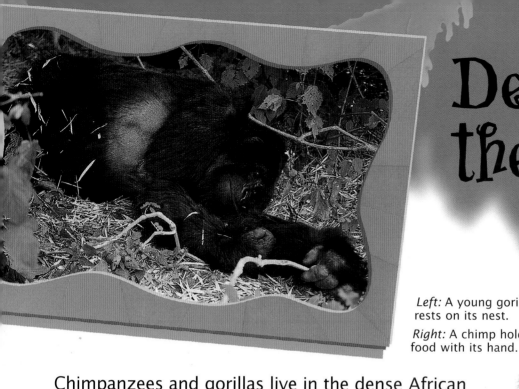

Left: A young gorilla rests on its nest.

Right: A chimp holds food with its hand.

Chimpanzees and gorillas live in the dense African forests. One reason they do well there is because of their thumbs. Most apes and monkeys have thumbs—like people do—so they can grab on to things. Chimps use their hands to make tools. They crack open nuts by pounding them with rocks. They'll even push a stick deep inside a termite mound and pull out bugs to slurp up.

Chimps and gorillas know what it means to "make your bed." Every day they make a new nest from branches and leaves, and curl up for a snooze.

Isn't It Wild?

Africa's largest snake, the rock python, slithers and slides through African forests. These pythons can grow to be 30 feet long and weigh over 100 pounds. They overcome prey as large as a wildebeest by squeezing it. After eating such a large meal, a python can go months —even a year— before eating again!

Above: A leopard hangs out in a tree.

A leopard's tan coat and dark spots blend in with trees and keep it well hidden in the forest. Leopards are good swimmers and incredible climbers. They'll drag their meal—often an animal twice their size—way up into a tree. There it's safe from other animals...and the leopard can enjoy the leftovers for days.

7

On the Waterfront

The river is a good home for hippos. A hippopotamus can weigh as much as 8,000 pounds! It's hard to believe that such large animals are good swimmers, but the water easily supports their huge bodies. A hippo's eyes, ears, and nose are toward the top of its head and stay above the water's surface. So even when hippos are mostly under-water they know what's going on around them.

Another pair of eyes just above the water's surface belongs to the crocodile. A crocodile's strong tail helps it zip through the water. It can stay underwater for an hour!

Above: The hippo has a huge mouth.

Flamingos live on lakes and salty lagoons in which most other animals can't survive. A flamingo holds its head upside down and scoops up small shrimp and *algae* (tiny plants) from the water. This food source has huge amounts of vitamin A, which gives flamingos their bright pink color.

Right: Flamingos have very flexible necks.

Below: A crocodile pauses at water's edge.

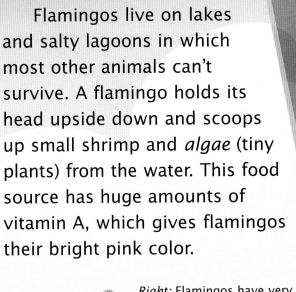

Isn't It Wild?

A pelican scoops fish into its large pouch and swallows them whole. They can eat 4 pounds of fish a day. A pelican's beak can hold up to 3 gallons of water!

The Dry Desert

Another desert animal is the meerkat, which is a type of *mongoose*, a small weasel-like animal. Meerkats take turns keeping an eye out for danger. A meerkat will stand up on its back legs and scan the area around it. When hunting it will keep its nose to the ground, sniffing out mice, ants, and scorpions to eat.

The desert is hot and dry, and camels are built for desert living. The wide flat shape of their feet keeps them from sinking into the sand. A camel's hump does not contain water, it stores fat. This fat is used for energy during lean times. But camels can go for days without food and water.

Above: The African camel has one hump.
Right: A group of meerkats keeps watch.

And speaking of eating insects, bat-eared foxes have such good hearing that they can hear bugs moving underground. They pinpoint where the bugs are, dig them up, and chow down.

Ostriches are also able to live in dry areas. They peck at the ground and find seeds, insects, and small reptiles for their meal. Ostriches eat grasses, and leaves from trees and bushes. And although they can't fly, ostriches can run up to 40 mph. They are the largest birds in the world!

Isn't It Wild?

One ostrich egg weighs 5 pounds. That's about what 24 chicken eggs weigh—which would add up to lots of omelets! Ostrich parents gently turn the eggs over in the nest several times a day, so that the chick inside each egg doesn't get stuck on one side of the shell while it grows.

Above: An ostrich watches over her eggs.

Lean on Me

There are many ways that one animal's behavior helps other animals. Giraffes are the tallest animals in the world, and other animals count on them to see danger first. So when giraffes run away, animals such as zebras and gazelles follow them and run too. This gives the animals a good head start on their enemies.

Oxpeckers are birds that will hitch a ride on the back of a giraffe or rhinoceros.

Above: A rhino with oxpeckers on its back.

The birds pick bugs and dirt off the animal's skin and get a good meal in return. But for the rhino, these birds do an extra good deed. Rhinos have very poor eyesight. When danger is near, the birds fly away and chatter. This lets the rhino know that something is up.

Left: Oxpeckers clean a young giraffe's skin.

Below: A croc shows off its clean teeth.

Isn't It Wild?

Crocodiles have their own little toothbrushes. Plover birds pick at a croc's teeth for leftover food. The plovers get fed, and the crocodile gets a dazzling smile!

Giraffes can grow as tall as 19 feet. But a giraffe has only seven vertebrae, or bones, in its neck. That's the same amount a person has. Each giraffe vertebra is 8 inches high—that's ten times bigger than ours! Giraffes also have the largest eyes of any land animal and can see clearly for miles.

Keep on Trekkin'

You may have heard of birds that *migrate*, or travel long distances to warmer weather and then back again. Did you know that some African animals also migrate?

A wildebeest is a weird-looking antelope with an oxlike head. During the dry season millions of wildebeests travel hundreds of miles for grass and water. They can cover 30 miles in one day. Traveling with the wildebeest are zebras and gazelles. They all follow rain clouds and lightning in the distance, knowing relief from dry weather is up ahead.

Above: Wildebeests travel in a large group.

Right: Thompson's gazelles have a black stripe on their side.

These migrating animals face many dangers along the way. Deep water, hungry lions and crocodiles, and tiredness are just a few of their problems. Zebras stay safer by keeping together. They will move at the pace of their slowest family member. This way no one is left behind. If a baby zebra gets lost in the herd, it can find its mother because it knows what her stripes look like.

After these migrating animals eat and graze for a few months, the rains will have returned to their homeland. It's time for them to head back and begin all over again.

Right: A herd of zebras stops for a drink.

Isn't It Wild?

Male wildebeests do something very brave that no other antelopes do. When hunted, they will stay behind the group or stumble to act hurt to get the attention of a hungry lion or hyena. While this is happening, the rest of the wildebeest group has time to run away.

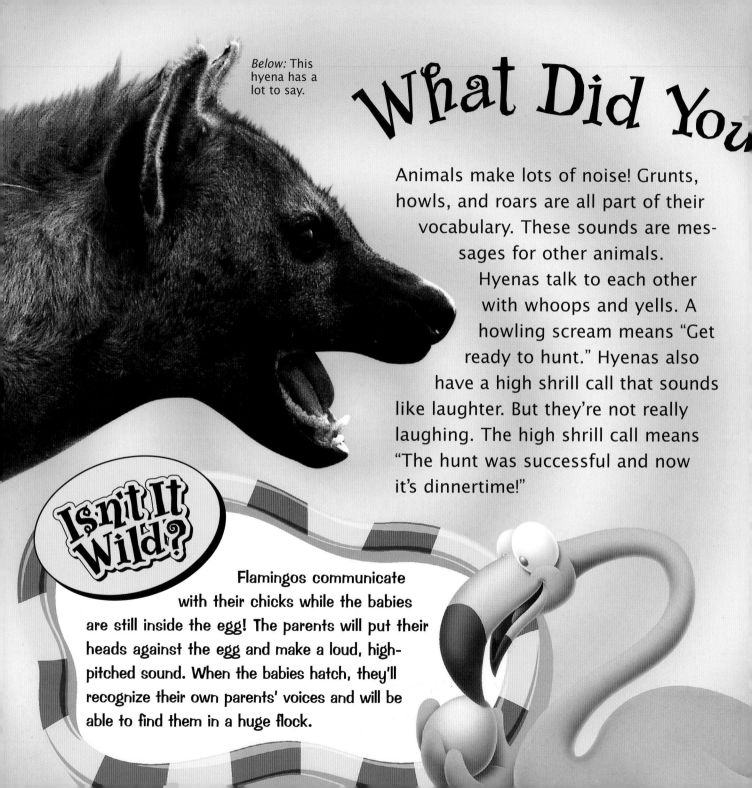

Below: This hyena has a lot to say.

Animals make lots of noise! Grunts, howls, and roars are all part of their vocabulary. These sounds are messages for other animals.

Hyenas talk to each other with whoops and yells. A howling scream means "Get ready to hunt." Hyenas also have a high shrill call that sounds like laughter. But they're not really laughing. The high shrill call means "The hunt was successful and now it's dinnertime!"

Isn't It Wild?

Flamingos communicate with their chicks while the babies are still inside the egg! The parents will put their heads against the egg and make a loud, high-pitched sound. When the babies hatch, they'll recognize their own parents' voices and will be able to find them in a huge flock.

Say?

Right: Chimps express many feelings.

A chimp can make more than 30 different sounds and many faces. When a chimp shows its teeth, it looks like a smile. But the chimp is really saying it's afraid. When a male gorilla beats his chest, it is often to let other gorillas know he's boss. Elephants communicate across many miles with a sound so low people can't hear it.

Baboons, which live in groups called troops, have a whole lot to say to each other. While playing, they'll grunt and chatter, and they'll screech when afraid. Troop members know to listen for an alarm bark given by a baboon leader. It's a warning that an enemy, such as a leopard, is nearby.

Right: A male gorilla beats his chest.

Family Ties

While animals such as the rhinoceros and the leopard like to live alone, others depend a lot on each other. Elephant herds can be made up of mothers, babies, sisters, aunts, grandmothers, cousins, and some males. They all look out for one another. If one elephant is sick, others will walk on either side of it, protecting it from their enemies.

Below: Traveling together, an elephant family keeps close bonds.

Giraffes help each other out by baby-sitting. When adult giraffes go to find food, their young wait at "home." They stay in a group called a *kindergarten*. Some female giraffes will stay behind with them until the other moms come back.

Some animals don't live in herds but share home duties with one another. Black eagles are family-oriented, and will stay with one mate for life. When there are eggs in the nest, the father sits on them during the day, taking turns with the mother. He also takes over all the hunting duties from the mother for weeks after the chicks are hatched.

Above: A black eagle carries a twig back to its nest.

Left: Adult giraffes protect their young at a watering hole.

Isn't It Wild?

Will crocodile eggs become boys or girls? It all depends on the temperature! If a croc's nest is too cold, the eggs will hatch with only females inside. If it's too hot, most of them will be females. If the temperature is in the middle, all the babies will be male.

A-Hunting We Will Go

Above: A cheetah chases down prey.

Animals who hunt other animals for food are called *predators*. They need to be very skilled to survive the hard life in the wild. Cheetahs are amazing predators because they're the fastest animals on land. A cheetah can go from zero to 45 mph in just 2 seconds and can reach speeds of 60 mph. Cheetahs will give it their all for about a minute, then they'll have to rest before running again.

Cape hunting dogs hunt together in large groups called packs. They are the only predators that let their young eat before the adults. Cape hunting dogs also bring back food to old and sick dogs that can't hunt anymore.

Gazelles, like all antelopes, are not hunters; they are the hunted. So it's a good thing they can run fast, make sharp turns, and zigzag quickly. Gazelles don't eat meat, but graze on grasses and bushes. They always stay alert for lions, cheetahs, hyenas, and Cape hunting dogs.

Above: This gazelle is alert for hunters.
Below: Cape hunting dogs gather in a pack.

Isn't It Wild?

Vultures are nature's cleanup crew! When predators finish eating, vultures swoop in and eat the leftovers. This cleanup plays a very important role in nature. When eating leftovers from the same animal, each vulture has a different job. Some tear, some peck, and some get the "crumbs."

21

Endangered Animals

Elephants, cheetahs, gorillas, chimps, rhinoceroses, and crocodiles are all endangered. That means as time goes on there are fewer and fewer of them. There are many reasons for this. People need more room and are building on wide-open spaces and cutting down forests where animals live. Elephants are hunted for their two ivory teeth called tusks, while rhinos are hunted for their horns. People must find ways to stop harming animals and the places they live before these animals become extinct, or totally die out.

The good news is, some changes are happening. Land has been set aside as reserves where endangered animals are protected and can live more safely.

Centers are being built to care for animals that have been hurt or abandoned. A lot of countries, including the United States, have also made laws against importing ivory. Zoos all over the world now have programs to protect endangered animals, too. All of these things are helping to give endangered animals a better chance for survival.

Animal Reserve

Isn't It Wild?

To protect wildlife in Africa, Kenya set aside hundreds of square miles of land at the foot of the famous snow-topped Mt. Kilimanjaro. Known as Amboseli National Park, the reserve might look dry and dusty, but it gets a constant supply of water from underground streams fed by the mountain's melting snow. Now, more than 900 elephants, some with the largest tusks in all of Kenya, make Amboseli their home.

Animal Antics!

Here are some cool things for you to make and do with the toy African animals. Household items you may need include scissors, a marker, a pencil, washable ink, construction paper, an 8 ½" x 14" sheet of paper, dried beans, a ruler, 32 paper cups, 16 small pieces of paper, toilet-paper tube or paper-towel roll, tinfoil, masking tape, an empty coffee can or oatmeal box with lid, tape, and two spring-type clothespins.

MEET A CHEETAH

Make a cool-looking cheetah to keep you company. First gather a pencil, construction paper, scissors, a ruler, glue, and two spring-type clothespins.

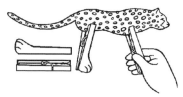

Drawing the cheetah: Using the toy animal as a model, draw and cut out 4 legs with paws, the same length as the clothespins. Then draw and cut out the cheetah's body, tail, and head (all in one piece, about 6″ long).

Building the cheetah: Glue the legs on each side of the spring-type clothespins. The paws should be at the smooth end of the clothespins. Then clip the legs to the body of the cheetah—and it's ready to stand up!

MATCH GAME

Challenge your memory! You'll need 32 paper cups and 16 small pieces of paper. Play alone or with a friend.

Setting up: Number the bottoms of the cups, giving each one a number from 1–32. Then, on the small pieces of paper, write the name of each type of toy animal (see inside front cover of book). Put a toy animal or piece of paper under each cup. Mix up the cups. Place the cups in four rows of eight.

Playing the game: Try to match the animal with its name by calling out any two numbers. Then lift up the cups, and see if it's a match. If it is, you can turn over the cups and keep the toy animal. If it's not a match, turn the cups over again, leaving the toy animal under its cup. Have the next person take a turn. The player who ends up with the most toy animals is the winner. If you play alone, time yourself and see how quickly you can match them all!

SPOT THE GIRAFFE

Every giraffe has a different pattern of spots. Each one is unique, just like your fingerprints. Here is a way to create your own special spotted giraffe. First, gather construction paper, a marker, and washable ink.

Drawing your giraffe: Using your toy animal as a model, draw a picture of a giraffe. Make it as tall as your sheet of paper. Just draw the outline; don't color it in.